A Pocketful of Chalk

Claire Booker

ARACHNE PRESS

First published in UK 2022 by Arachne Press Limited
100 Grierson Road, London, SE23 1NX
www.arachnepress.com
© Claire Booker 2022

ISBNs
Print: 978-1-913665-69-2
eBook: 978-1-913665-70-8

The moral rights of the author have been asserted.

All rights reserved. This book is sold subject to the condition that it shall not, by way of trade or otherwise, be lent, resold, hired out or otherwise circulated without the publisher's prior written consent in any form or binding or cover other than that in which it is published and without similar condition including this condition being imposed on the subsequent purchaser.

Except for short passages for review purposes no part of this publication may be reproduced, stored in a retrieval system or transmitted in any form or by any means, electronic, mechanical, photocopying, recording or otherwise, without prior written permission of Arachne Press.

Thanks to Muireann Grealy for her proofreading.

Cover design © Fiona Humphrey

Acknowledgements

These poems (or versions of them) first appeared in the following publications.

An Osprey Fledges, Dinosaur Boy, Channel (issue 5);
Anniversary, Walking the Edge, Loose Muse anthologies (Spring 2013, Autumn 2013);
Breaking Out, First Kiss, Structo (issue 20);
Drone Boys, Museum of Childhood, The Spectator (2020);
Fisherman's Daughter, Bringing in the Fruit, Mr McGregor's Seedlings, Solstice Shorts anthologies 2019, 2020, 2021 (Arachne Press);
Footprints, Artemis (issue 27);
Framed Woman, The Poetry Society Website (runner-up, 2021 Stanza Competition);
Gaia in the Back Garden, Caduceus (issue 107);
Gang, erbacce (issue 45);
Hey Diddle Diddle, Poetry Salzburg Review, (issue 38);
Italian Hair, Dreamcatcher (issue 40);
News Flash, The Morning Star (23rd Dec 2021);
Night Bus, Morning After, Bringing You Back, On the centenary of my teacups, The High Window (Summer 2016, Autumn 2019, Summer 2021);
On Beacon Hill, Poems on the Buses winner (Guernsey, 2018);
Paperwhite Narcissi, Fossil Fish, Pennine Platform (issue 91)
Remembering Chocolate, South (issue 45);
Sand: Naming the Parts, I think of rain and it's you, Stand (vol 20 – 1);
Skewed, The Rialto (issue 88);
The Wrasse, Poetry Birmingham Literary Journal (issue 7);
Turning Back, Lunar Pareidolia, Finished Creatures (issues 3 & 5);
The Invitation, Prole (issue 8);
The Lightness of Words, Grey Heron, Spelt (issues 1 & 4);
Towards Beachy Head, Sussex Wildlife Trust online anthology 'Awakenings' 2021.
Waiting for Glory, New Welsh Review (multi-media film, 2015);

My gratitude also to Mimi Khalvati, Lisa Kelly, Jane Maker, Alan Price, Marion Tracy, Caroline Vero, The Brighton Stanza Group, Live Cannon and The Poetry Kit for their invaluable feedback on a number of these poems.

Last, but not least, my sincere thanks to Cherry Potts at Arachne Press for making this collection possible.

To Jayne D-T

In warm appreciation of your insight and care.

Also by Claire Booker

The Bone That Sang
(Indigo Dreams Publishing, 2020)

Later There Will Be Postcards
(Green Bottle Press, 2016*)*

A Pocketful of Chalk

Contents

Notes	8
Breaking Out	9
Looking Towards Smock Mill	10
Drone Boys	11
Call of Nature	12
Paperwhite Narcissi	13
Moon Kill	14
Hey Diddle Diddle . . .	15
Long Man Dreaming	16
Skewed	17
Sand: Naming the Parts	18
Bringing You Back	19
First Kiss	20
The Horse in My Bedroom	21
Museum of Childhood	22
Remembering Chocolate	23
Anniversary	24
Night Bus	25
On the centenary of my teacups	26
Italian Hair	27
Waiting for Glory	28
Towards Beachy Head	29
Morning After	30
Dinosaur Boy	31
Grey Heron	32
The Wrasse	33
Fisherman's Daughter	34
Framed Woman	36

An Osprey Fledges	37
Walking the Edge	38
I think of rain, and it's you	39
The Invitation	40
Turning Back	42
Lightness of Words	43
Gang	44
News Flash	45
Footprints	46
Lunar Pareidolia	47
Fossil Fish	48
On Beacon Hill	49
Bringing in the Fruit	50
Mr McGregor's Seedlings	51
Gaia in the Back Garden	52
Mirabelles	53
Green Ray	54

Notes

Long Man Dreaming: The Long Man of Wilmington is a chalk giant carved into the Sussex Downs. He's been refurbished with concrete blocks.

The Wrasse: Most wrasse are born female. Some transform into males at maturity.

Framed Woman: After *Cape Cod Morning* by Edward Hopper.

Footprints: The longest known trackway of human footprints is in White Sands, New Mexico. It was made over 10,000 years ago and is remarkable for its length (1.5km) and straightness.

Breaking Out

I've had it with full stops   planning endings
before they've even begun

I want a moonless night   scrumping for stars
Andromeda   the Pleiades   bruised
and juicy in my trug   to sink a fence post
into concrete   and watch wetness turn

I'm sick of weighing the word   I want
a Marbled White to burn my eyes with its
impossible exactness
                my hands to be coppered
      by the ear-splitting resin of marigolds

Give me the sea in conversation
with itself
                a wood-propped yew
with its bell-clap of crows   my fingertips
          dipped in rainwater nests

 I can't afford an hour to take   a comma out
              I'd rather ease up a dandelion
follow
the tap root down   into worm and grit
           where root-hairs go nodal
and even a fraction missed   will
                          burst
into sun clocks.

Looking Towards Smock Mill

Evening shadows make monsters of sheep.
Even a crow has its life stretched.
The sun raises me up like a beanstalk –
sends my head grazing on the slope opposite.

Here, beside the witch tree's propped stones,
I'm transcribed by light, and elevation.
My flint bones and wormy flesh breathe
effortlessly across chalk and tilth.

My sister the smock mill looks out to sea
with her dark arms flung.
I'm Stilt Woman, Giantess of the Hill.
If I turn, I'll vanish.

I could peel my whole length, roll me
under my arm as a keepsake.
Never before have I covered so much ground.
I let myself float in the beaks of birds.

Drone Boys

A van and two jeeps have rough-tracked down to where
    everything ends in slope and sky –

beer-cracking lads in the belly of the valley,
    unkegging their bladders against the one bent tree.

A light breeze lobs their heavy-metal blare
    and boisterous pant-hoots into the innocent pasture.

The cash crop here bleats on dark stalks: their tails jumpy
    as catkins, their shoulders numbered.

A drone revs up. A second joins it, slicing out territory
    over the struts of the burned-out barn.

They circle for a wider curettage, herd space, scythe
    the air with their waspish under-hangs,

come lower still, until the field erupts in unstoppable bleating,
    as if the chalk hill has grown lungs.

Every lamb is trying to cry itself back inside the womb.
    Their mothers stand like boulders – reply in deep baritone

from black mechanical mouths, udders triggered
    against the raptors' shrieking blades.

Call of Nature

A wise old ewe (she's weathered some winters)
watches me pee, square on to the intrigue.

I watch the amber bluster under the bridge
of my legs. It disappears into

this once in a lifetime scrim of grassy chalk.
When I rise with a zip she's still there.

Must I explain to this old dame – whose droppings
lie scattered in piles of liquorice,

her fleece lime-scale wet from a nonchalant bladder –
must I explain the pulling up of jeans?

I unzip. Whip up a moon haka. Flash her the flags
of my bare buttocks.

When I turn again, she's udders hindmost,
lips slowly winnowing grass.

Paperwhite Narcissi

I want to give you these little gods. I found them, wild
and stray in the back woods. Their wily scent
has brought my kitchen to a standstill. Though I've scoured,
stacked, mopped and scrubbed, I still can't wipe away

the guile of your mouth, punch drunk on mine –
the way we sank into that long surrender. This wanting
is too new an ache, too rash a fall. How I envy the cool
indifference of these voiceless hostages,

their heads tipped back, light trapped in their beaks.
Where do they keep their sensual hearts?
What blissful vertigo – to quench the burn of your touch
in their green reflective water. Or spiral

down each delicate carpel and hang on clusters
of moist seeds – almost weightless.

Moon Kill

milk-faced
perched on her nest of constellations

an owl
scoops through stars sharp as claw tips

the final moment
turns

on a
pin

Hey Diddle Diddle...

*No national space agency has plans to send a cow
into the void* – Wikipedia

Gazing from my nursery window, it used to worry me –
that clash of milky spheres. Would I hear udders slap
against moon rock? Where would she land?

Once on a Sussex scarp, I watched a heifer almost touch
the waning crescent as it sailed across day like a gasp.
She arched her back in a reckless act of optimism,
straining to launch herself over the barbed wire and up
towards new possibilities, more luminous than chalk.

Was she dreaming of the lunar veldts,
where she might graze unmolested by flies on the shores
of Mare Vaporum?

It's anybody's sky, but hoof-prints
in moon crust won't satisfy the nay-sayers.

I like to think hers was a giant leap for bovinekind.
That she back-flipped the Kármán line into a whoosh
of solar wind and atomic helium, gazed at our half-eclipsed
blue planet and took one small step into a fresh narrative.
There are no abattoirs on the moon.

Long Man Dreaming

Fish-tail clouds swim between my car wipers
rain pools swishing   back and forth   quick, quick, slow.
I pull up and park at the foot of the giant.

He's watching the heavens for weather
fierce in his newly breeze-blocked body   thoughts lost
in the transparency   flying with geese.

Inside the carburetor   petrol chatters
its abrasive dialect of long-dead foliage. We sink
into blue haze. A brook has begun to babble

through my head. The leather seats are growing
back their bones. The walnut dashboard   sways   gives shade.
Fish will inherit the earth   booms the giant

as he sluices against currents with his upright poles
transformed into oars. They slap, slap between drowning
steeples   tractors floating belly-up   corpses

swept along in huddled herds. A mackerel shoots
rainbows across the car bonnet. Lobsters have tethered
themselves to the Pay & Display.

Their bubbles scatter like petulant bullets.
I rummage for my parking coins   find flint stones.
Is it too late to buy a ticket?

Skewed

Silhouetted on the ridge, single claw raised against the sun,
it turns from bungalows nesting pinkly in the dip,

attacks the long flounce of field draped to the copse.
Only when a cloud swabs the soil, do I see yellow wheels

and a shirt that must be the driver.
Less than half the field is tilled, wheat stubble jittering

in the wind. The drill-bit judders and starts to bite
out a line, winces against the angles.

It's planting seagulls – great squabbling rows.
At each turn, the white gash erupts, mobs the glittering cabin.

A local woman stops to bag up after her dachshund.
He never gets his lines straight. Look at the kink in that.

She tells me he only ploughs on Sundays.
The rest of the week, he hammers out dents in stock cars.

The tractor presses on, like a great scarab –
its dung balls in the next field, waiting to be collected.

Sand: Naming the Parts

On my fingertip, a single dab of the multiverse that glistens from newly retreated brine.

These gritty specks mosaic my skin, turn me
into a splinter of night, a causeway of nebulae
quilted, inflated, quantum, cyclic.
I begin to notice how the young hot stars
I call my own replicate themselves, cell by cell,
in this great translation of matter.

The sea cries out to its little works of art –

> *black rib, razor (blue), golden hornet, triskele,*
> *brick bit, razor (white), vase chip, golden ear, trapezium* ~

waves suck at the shore lumber:
smashed chalk, flint fists, cobbles like cannon balls
gravid with future sand, each one ruminating its history
of impacts – volcanoes, meteor hits, honey/white dents.
Such a skirl of atoms, a molecular dip-paddle
into the condensed pandemonium of time.

A child waddles past, lugging infinity in a bucket.

> *brick bit (II), staghorn, red speck, golden torque, brick bit (III)*
> *heartspoon, elver (grey), cromlech, feather, flake,*
> *black scrap (V)*

The grains on my finger are becoming endless.

Bringing You Back
i.m. Aryamati

A sheaf of poems, signed in your careful hand.
I sit, holding your Tibetan Vajra bell,

a single candle lit. No longer ballasted
with breath or bone, you surface

from the flimsy dark
strung magically on your own notes.

The months disperse, like a sea mist lifting.
Those mornings I followed you

further and further out along the spit,
your diminishing form

stooped in awe of shells I crushed
without seeing.

You wrapped your words in paper.
How freely you offer them to me now.

First Kiss

Autumn has a way with light, prolonging space,
making horizons sail achingly close.
A landslip of sights greets me from the top of Folly Hill.

Georgian brickwork,
the castle keep, clouds pinned by steeples –
the gasworks, an ugly thumb print.

Behind me, bracken sprawls its cinnabar pelt,
still warm with the possibility of adders.
It's a long walk along flint walls

to the swallow holes where we banjaxed
our sled one winter-stiff Christmas,
planted an apple pip, glimpsed the mythical stoat.

When the school bell tolls, it's calling other lives.
The weather vane's still undecided: *North, East, South
and West, who is the boy that I love best?*

Somewhere, I'll find an oak that keeps the hoop
of my arms in its memory – a girl on the brink,
practising al fresco kissing on one such flimsy day.

The Horse in My Bedroom

Those days of first magic –
my flick-book
a pivot of creation.
Let there be life, I said,
and life woke
to my touch: a white horse
thundered
through my fingers,
more alive to me
than all those beasts
hemmed in by flesh and fences.
Its ribs were tensile as bellows,
the mane drilled back,
gather and stretch of eager hocks.
I never tired of setting it free
into its wilderness
of lines and stippled paper.
When I ran out of pages, it petrified
into a quire of twenty stallions,
stabled and silent.

Museum of Childhood

The little dictionary lies open at *A for Apple*
where it all begins. I want to turn

the pages, but the vitrine is a border crossing,
my ageing face, stamped on its glass,

my papers way out of date.
Moths have been at work along the faded pink

of a rabbit's ear. It's swiveled to catch lost sounds.
A big, red button reads: *PRESS ME*. So I do,

and the little train clatters along N-gauge tracks,
disappears into the papier-mâché tunnel.

A long heart-skip, before it emerges still guarding
its secret: the dark curved space,

a pin prick of light dilating like an amazed pupil
at the approaching world.

Remembering Chocolate

I meet the glaze in my father's eyes.
Are you the new nurse? he hazards, one hand adrift
behind the pillow. It seems easiest to nod –
swallow my name under a starched smile.

Cellophane rustles around the chocolate rabbit
I've brought him. I place it carefully on the bed.
Happy Easter, I say, wishing him dead.

Is it? You know?
Yes.
You know . . . that brown thing, you know . . .
Chocolate, I offer.

He takes the word as a gift, tugs at the ribbon
with his engineer's fingers, then plunders the bow.
I watch his mouth smear with joy.

That face tips me back into the plush velvet
of The Adelphi. On stage, a tiny speck of light is dying,
but I can't bring myself to lie. I turn
to find my father evangelical in his clapping: *Yes, I believe
in fairies. Don't let Tinkerbell die!*

Later, when I'm clearing out his locker,
I'll find the Easter rabbit – its snapped off head
meticulously twined onto fragments of body
by a slender thread of crimson ribbon.

Anniversary

To lose a loved one implies a lack of care,
a mislaid item somewhere waiting.

Inevitably, words let us down.

Many times I've passed Lost Property
tempted to enquire.

This morning, I dropped by,
gave them your description:

*about so high, slightly bent with age,
wonderfully musical.*

They brought out a trombone.

Night Bus

You're wedged on the aisle side
all breath'd up from the rush for a seat,
blocked by a blether of faces.

In a moment, you'll see me.

A veiled woman holds her baby
to the window. I float through this icon
attempting to catch your eye.

The baby pat-a-cakes my reflection,
mouths something profound.

As the bus throttles up,
your face begins its fragile journey of turning
towards me.

On the centenary of my tea cups

I get to thinking of mouths.
People who sipped on roses, their lips

skating fine bone china.
So many tongues passing time

in the orbit of these fragile moons.
Weddings, wars, wakes, unpacked, re-packed,

into which sideboard,
awaiting which removal van?

A century of ritual has scuffed their gilded rims,
like pilgrims hollowing cathedral steps.

Tide upon tide of lives engraved –
ebb and flow of small eclipses.

Italian Hair

My aunt always claimed Italian hair made the best wigs,
went doolally over Sophia Loren's pulsating coiffure,
Monica Vitti's curtain of polished keratin, everything
and anything about Lollobrigida,

whilst her own under-achieving barnet
was lacquered, sprayed, back-combed and pumped up
like a Norfolk turkey – yet still never got to wade
through the Trevi Fountain.

I think of her as I'm stuck behind Italian students
sing-songing along the undercliff walk to Brighton.
They seem unimpressed by the slate sea, damp shingle,
granite Marina louring ahead.

But their hair. Bella figura in ravishing handfuls.
A harvest of earth, terracotta, sun, sculpted with pins
or levitating in the wind, flaunted on this impromptu
catwalk back-lit by brash white cliff.

My aunt finally got her wig. An NHS nylon number,
more Nora Batty than Claudia Cardinale. But she worked it
with rollers and tongs, made it earn its passage.
Her hair grew back, wiry and grey, still dreaming of Tuscany.

Waiting for Glory

The bell tower strikes the quarter hour.
Dandelion clocks are tonsured: gibbous, sickle
to blind stub. Their seeds rise on a waft
of wild garlic and swaying dock –

break free from the corral of stooping graves.
A may bush, dowager-bent,
has flung its bouquet backwards,
shoots thorn and cream-cupped scent.

Starlings rout in screech and clack
up slipways of a monstrous yew.
Buried under the clamber of boy-high cleavers,
Obadiah Legg, aged 67, waits for glory.

Towards Beachy Head

The purple smoke of wild thyme has blown
these windswept hills awake. Sky above scarp, sheep
buttoned on grass or flopped against thorn –
lambs, stained prophetic red, butt at the teat.

Air turns skittish blue with butterflies.
They mate on ox-eye daisies, flit the thin sinew
of life for flung bounty on either side.
Two buzzards slow spiral. Their mew, mew

spills flocks of finches from invisible wire.
White triangles are inching along a swatch of sea.
Cliff top boys stop. Squint up. Higher and higher,
a lark unravels its song, seamlessly.

Morning After

The moon's a stone that's sunk
way under, peeling the tide on automatic.

Cormorants hoist black sails, suck on sun, dive.
This is how to fish, beaks scissoring

fat pieces of mottle and rainbow.
On the beach, deckchairs preen and flutter.

Children skedaddle, relentlessly harvesting day.
No whisper about last night's

brimstone party of scorched spume, the shoreline
buttock bare in sea spew,

oyster shuck, crab carapace.
When drunken clouds raged biblical

in a smashed blood-yolk sky, and marauders
glided their Jurassic silhouettes west.

Dinosaur Boy

When we arrive, the sea's still beating out
thunderous footsteps. You greet the cliff with ballyhoos
and a small hammer. You're our chest-high
recruiting sergeant, drilling us in that compulsive

stock-taking you've made your own. You try
Brachiosaurus and *Triceratops* for the zing of ancient flesh
on your tongue; snap and ketch in crazy zig zag
among spume-sticky fusillades

hurled by nine-footers during last night's gale.
Pebbles come alive in your hands. *Flint eggs* you call them,
nesting them tight against your chest. We smash them
for their innards like demented crows.

You're Jacques Cousteau, cracking the depths in your air-
tight helmet whilst we, your able seamen, merely
slacken the ropes, marvel as your head crackles in oceans
far beyond us, letting monsters come up for air.

Grey Heron

God of pond.
God of the turning tide
and garnished rock pools.
Every day is Judgement Day
under my unfurled cloak.
Water here edged harder than rock.
Rain on the lash. A swirl
of purled whites, jumping greens.
Two throatfuls of frog.
Still as a bulrush, ear on the skew,
I throw no shadow.
Flash, stab. Blood, salt.
My neck stacks, unstacks, restacks.
Twig-beaked atop a tree,
I watch her fly –
legs a trail of sticks,
instincts weaving wild.
When she flattens her back,
we become one cluster, one parade
of wings.
Nest. Nest. Nest.
We'll plug it with eggs,
small beaks gulping for sky-fish.

The Wrasse

She fell for his line –
the jabbed-on bait like a star in sky-water.
Now she lies in the crib
of his capable hands: a jig hook
deep in her gullet, all fight left in a sea
that spits against the groynes.

I stop by the stockade of rods
to watch his calm work with pliers.
He's shielded the gills
with kitchen paper; squints
into her throat, inserts gently and deeper.
But still the hook won't yield.

*It's bass we're after. Our quota's
one a day. The boats take all they want. No limit.*
His mate is bullish, sits eyes hooked
to his own slack line, casts again
into the wriggling sack of sea – dreams
of a beauty hanging plumb

to the drop, stiff fins fighting.
Would it help if I held her?
The angler flings me a smile, puts down
his pliers in no kind of rush.
It's an awkward pause. He faces away.
Gives a single, well-aimed punch.

Fisherman's Daughter

Dad was an artist with a needle –
woosh, woosh it would go, like Sunday rain
and I'd lie in bed listening to him
mending or making.

Nets came straight from the beach,
strung on a hook by our hearth, and he'd braid
right there, on a big old bedspread
between Mum's dresser and the pull-out table,

unhitching stories
until the room started rocking like a beamer
and I could smell the fish shoaling,
feel their weight as they pulled against the trawl,

bubbles breaking.
You could say I made a good catch, but
it was strange that first dawn with Bill lying
beside me: not a sound from downstairs,

as if the house had stopped breathing.
I still miss Dad's sure hands tightening the twine,
and his quiet ear for my life.
He was never one to tie on a smile,

but none of my worries
were too small to fling back and we'd sit for hours
looping and twisting the rows.
Dad called it cutting the holes out.

Once the little 'uns arrived, I knew
there'd be no hole big enough to wriggle through.
Fish don't know how to go backwards.
That's how it works.

Framed Woman

Somewhere in the kitchen
there will be mackerel or snapper,
boned and gutted on a plate,
their scales lying in predictable ranks.
This is the odour of her life.

She can't quite spoon herself out
of his crabshell house –
its pragmatic clapboard: so flat,
so regular, each slat casting
a thin blue shadow.

Her breasts are haltered
inside a home-sewn dress,
her hands welded to a table.
Panes of light frame
those pale arms, soft as roe.

She tries to shut out the pulse
of Atlantic rollers,
the taste of youth in her throat,
but a memory is ripening
under the cloche of his windows –

a tendril unlaces
in the white-hot sun.

An Osprey Fledges

this scoop   this mossy bowl   these jagged

battlements   and by the grace

talons gripping reef knots of sticks

inexplicable wings

rehearse the untried lightness

as if by decree or secret knowledge

diamonds shake on the ruff of her neck

she twists 180°   beaks the shrill sky

calling in an astounding new language

to kill   to feed   to mate

her eyes are embossed with a glint of fish

the great tiled arches flex   unflex   stretch heraldic

beat repeat-repeat against the drop   then up

into her inheritance

Walking the Edge

We trail bright verticals pocked with flint,
whiter than yarrow heads, whilst underfoot, lime
insinuates, eclipses my boot seams.

You in your impractical espadrilles uncoil your charm.
I see the pearl in your tongue,
catch a hint of cigarillo.

You gather me in, as I harvest rue for drying –
a fine crop. Your words, I think, will pass as migrant birds;
beautiful for a season. But you will be constant.

Not so. Those expert hands have weighed my flesh,
ground these yielding bones to raise your bread
and now you're slaked, you'll drop me

eternally laughing into your eighth collection –
muse an honourable estate: think Lizzie Siddal
to your Rossetti.

Think again.
I'll not be your bricked-in anchorite.
I am the countless beats that stir in this great cliff.

I think of rain, and it's you

apocalyptic,
tympanic on bins,
drenched beyond dreich, gone
before you arrive, on the slant, tensile, colour
of bitumen, biting, spitting, driving,
a wind-herded squall, drunk on isobars,
smell like green thunder,
like a car crash, like a direct hit,
a flick in the eye,
prismatic, on the wrong side of the court,
flimsy as commitment, like a withholding,
like the pearly nap of a lawn, sheets of you,
straight from the hip, flush as furrows,
a lip-smacked pond
O< O< O
skinny dipping in my pools,
barbeled as a cat fish, sun-prickled,
crop-wrecking, moon-
fellator, slick on the tongue,
feather-light, falling
in nano
drops
drip, drip

drip

drip

The Invitation

I remember your promise:
the meadow lands of Sussex laid out
before us like a picnic on best linen,
and talk of wild parties –

the way the gravel bruised my feet,
a slew of cars silting the driveway,
and how the Jacobean chimneys shifted
shape with each new angle.

Inside, old gherkin jars lit up the kitchen,
bright with split peas. Voices curled
like smoke along corridors. Gun dogs
sprawled on cracked tiles.

The night was full of door slam
and things half said, strangers touching
in corners, a girl draped in fox fur, swaying
through a room of clocks.

We slept on the floor wrapped
in patchouli and other people's snores,
the oak boards butting my hips
each time I turned, and you too spaced

to go beyond the perfunctory.
As day slid out from under night,
I rose in my Greek sandals,
passed waking lawns, topiary lions,

the ha-ha, an ornamental gate,
and watched an ancient hornbeam,
black with rooks,
fling hieroglyphs into the sky.

Now I see it was the last time
we would spend together wild –
and that, not wild enough
for a last time.

Turning back

I find myself entangled in red.
Crumpled bloody handkerchiefs of maple,
or maybe dogwood? It's a kind of folly,
this letting go – or a foretelling.

Light filters the carousel of aimless leaves
which crash against walls of eternal holly.
I hold out my hands to catch, but none
drop onto my supplicant palms –

only acorns pelting the ground.
Corrugated clay, thick as a kiss, has moated
the path. There's a gate ahead, half open,
the way reckless in snaking ivy.

I hesitate. The gate's half shut against me,
and my feet are bruised.

Lightness of Words

Here on the fell edge,
ripping up your letters, there's an infinity
of words to let go.

Shreds of paper writhe
like white snakes, lift from my fingers
on feral currents. Your promises,

plucked to the bone,
are lost to the pull of True North. Words crash
into ledges, scree, fists

of earth, lie disjointed on briar
and blackthorn, like divorcing couples asking:
did we ever love each other?

Gang

Walking The Level late at night,
shadows hunch ahead of me.

No footsteps but a sense of grip.
The stench of it.

A third, a fourth. The men grow leaner,
sharper, thin as blades.

Faster now, steps almost at a run.
Can I make it to the road?

Too late, a fifth, a sixth, a pack –
the power of the withheld punch.

Swing round. Give them eyes.
Above all eyes.

I turn.
Asphalt shines in night's rain.

Rows of lamp posts either side –
their shadows straight as broom handles.

News Flash

At The Fortune of War we soak up late October sun,
drink craft cider, anticipate the shots to come. *The Taliban
have beheaded a women's youth volleyball player.* Hubbub
at slatted tables, joggers blast past, kids happy-screaming,
hipsters on Segways. *The Taliban have beheaded a women's
youth volleyball player.* Seagulls dive bomb for chips, smash
plates, glasses, wild applause. *The Taliban have beheaded
a women's youth volleyball player.* The beach lies neck
down in pebbles; glint of Sunday kayakers. *The Taliban have
beheaded a women's youth volleyball player.* Girls tumble
in borrowed sand – lit up, laughing, aching with life's endlessness.
The Taliban have beheaded a women's youth volleyball player.

Footprints

She moves, quicksilver straight, across ancient saltpans
simmered to stone. Time has shaved her down

to the soles of her feet. I can hear her rasping for air.
A slip here, a stretch there: she's a woman,

in the rain, in a hurry. Her instep and arches talk by proxy
via scans and diagrams. A mile of fossil casts

tattooed into the strata. No deviation, a gauntlet of danger,
each step deepened by the weight of a child.

Twice, she put him down (we can tell). Was it to rest?
Her toddler is heavier than time itself. I can scoop him

from the half-light, absorb his warmth as he clutches for
comfort. I know the firm hook of her arm, the watchful eye.

Imprinted in white sand, her steps walk through every mother –
a fierce, unflinching love that won't rub out.

Lunar Pareidolia

I hold the moon up to the sun.
Light bends, turns corners, throws illusions.
I dust its face for prints.

Some can see a rabbit, an old man,
a goddess. I see the children we might have had.
They don't hear me. Sound travels

silently through this thin body of space.
They play in a city of faces: not lost,
not vanished.

Every particle of dust is breathing –
games of hide and seek in long extinct volcanoes,
a dream of astronauts and butterfly nets.

As light bleaches the stars away,
our children fall to earth as meteorites,
rusted and stone dry.

Fossil Fish

its mouth held mute by the rip-tide
        of 90 million years,
                body the length of my finger joint
wrapped in a caul of flint   a moment   broken
        mid-flow   just as your too frail bones
once floated unreachably
on our scan

On Beacon Hill

A kestrel unpleats
in a patch of violet sky, its mate

on the eggs somewhere
brooding. You walk in silence,

and like the farmer I count my stock,
eyes shaded, not for the man

you were, but for the we
we have become – our feet in rhythm,

mud muffling the ancient spine
that binds these hills.

Some call it a trudge,
the unsure footwork, chalk rubble

tricky as lime.
But I love the climb –

backwards always behind us,
forwards, always ahead.

Bringing in the Fruit

Our little tree is the height of a man –
scuffed with age, chain-mailed in spit-grey lichen.

We arrive when it's breaking into leaf.
It may be apple or pear, plum or

even peach. It may be barren. So we wait –
for bees, for sunlight.

Scanty blossoms start to unboll, white as cotton.
Sometimes a dove paddles in its branches,

fills them with cooing. The little tree drags its anchor
through dry and chalky soil. All we can do

is keep hosing through the rainless weeks. Tiny plum
embryos, green and hard, take up position

and begin to swell. They're like children
to us now – the loss of even one puts a scab on the day.

Some fall to knots of orange-rimmed slugs.
Some shrivel, some thrive.

A blackbird sprints towards the boom
of purple with a lascivious eye.

Mr McGregor's Seedlings

Rosy-faced Kilner jars twinkle from all points
of his kitchen – some things, at least, can be bottled.

He forks air into what has been achieved: his soft fruits
win prizes; their yield is the envy of the allotment.

The rub and tilth of soil possesses him –
its endless riddles invade his fingers.

He's dug a small pond by the lean-to where he rests
with his flask in the company of frogs,

reads up about poisoned bees, plundered peat bogs,
pesticides that strip the land of worms.

On weekdays, voices from the infant school hop over,
lively as crickets. Next month he'll give a talk,

take little pots to plant enthusiasms, unpack a sunflower
to show its eager heart.

Gaia in the Back Garden

I find her crouched, knees by her ears,
plump as a newt, jockeying
the little patch of earth, flinging soil
with her sky-blue trowel.

They're not doing anything, she cries –
her hand speckled with radish sprouts,
their flopped pods and ripped filaments
like mandrake children.

A week is a month in her world.
When I try to explain how life grows
slowly and magically, like the new baby
on his way, she tugs us both down.

Seed packets clack on sticks behind us.
We lie, soil-warmed and innocent
on the earth's teeming belly.
Shhh, she whispers, and we listen.

Mirabelles

Three have tumbled to the ground.
On the cusp of flame, they glow
as if the firebird, her feathers snarled
in overhanging branches, flew
down and nested in this flinty dirt.

Their tree's seed arrived a cappella
carrying the ghost of tribal home,
where monks grafted the first cultivar
and citizens of Metz and Nancy
still fête them in pastry and spirit.

Here, on this downland cut-through,
they lie as if in final sleep, though life's
hard stone is in them, its eye tooth
patient among chalk divots, horse dung,
spiky bramble sweetness.

Wind hugs the westward slope,
sends a back-to-school shiver along the lichway.
Sunlight breaches, drops
down, spins a web across their faces,
makes their cheeks dance.

The feral plum tree sings its wasted fruit among
thickets of elder and thorn.
No one passes by in this treasured land
of unthumbed wealth.
There's beauty in the squander.

Green Ray

We do as trees do, bend away from the wind.
Love is under every stone, and in our quiet breathing.
The sun's slow yolk hangs over the sea,
ignites each wisp of hair at your temples.

You, more precious still, because just now,
without the need to ask, you pulled a bloody splinter
from your childhood, placed it in
my cupped hands like a day-old chick.

The hurt's been curled and waiting
since you chose to make yourself unbreakable.
It seems I've only seen you through polished glass,
as if caught in cloud furrow, or tasting ice.

We're watching for the green ray.
A flash more apple flesh than green.
Illusory, so the science says: a moment already passed,
levitating from the deep.